The Martial Arts Book

by Laura Scandiffio
art by Nicolas Debon

annick press
toronto + new york + vancouver

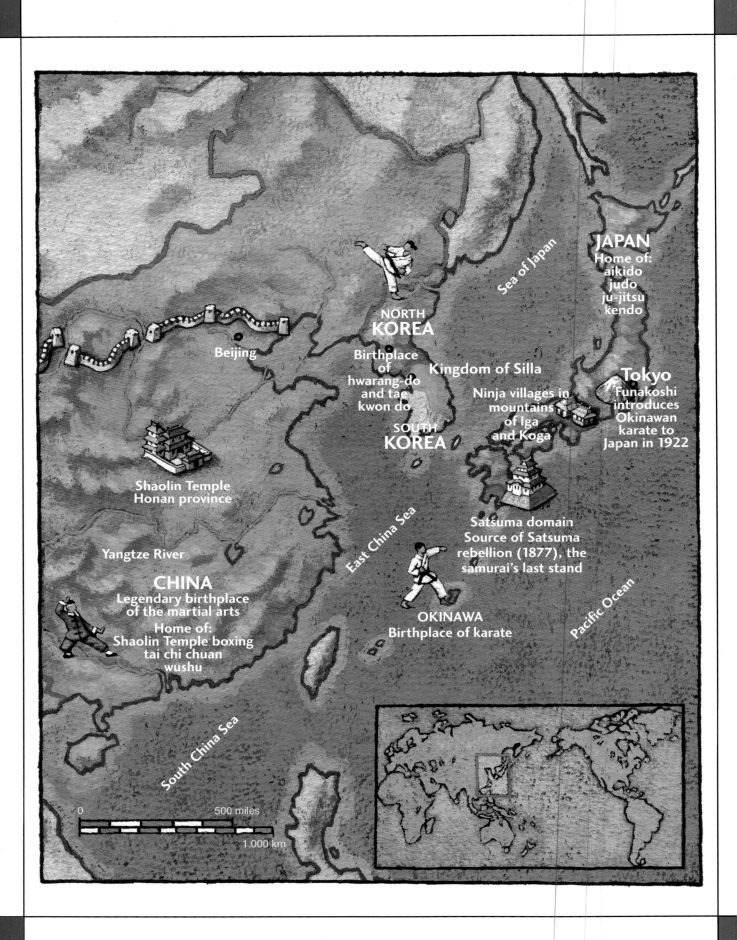

JAPAN
Home of:
aikido
judo
ju-jitsu
kendo

Sea of Japan

NORTH
KOREA

Beijing

Birthplace
of
hwarang-do
and tae
kwon do

Kingdom of Silla

Ninja villages in
mountains
of Iga
and Koga

Tokyo
Funakoshi
introduces
Okinawan
karate to
Japan in 1922

SOUTH
KOREA

Shaolin Temple
Honan province

Yangtze River

East China Sea

Satsuma domain
Source of Satsuma
rebellion (1877), the
samurai's last stand

CHINA
Legendary birthplace
of the martial arts
Home of:
Shaolin Temple boxing
tai chi chuan
wushu

OKINAWA
Birthplace of karate

Pacific Ocean

South China Sea

0   500 miles

1,000 km

Contents

What Are the Martial Arts?

When you think of the martial arts, what is the first thing that comes to mind? A movie actor or video-game hero defeating villains with flying kicks? Athletes in white uniforms winning gold medals? Or maybe learning to defend yourself against the neighborhood bully?

These may be some of the ways the martial arts have been used, but they have little to do with the true goals of a martial artist. So what are the real reasons for studying a martial art? The answers might surprise you.

Kung fu, karate, tae kwon do – there are many styles and different names, but they all have one thing in common. The first goal of training is to become the best person you can be.

And that means not just getting stronger and faster, but making the most of your mind and character, too. Masters of the martial arts believe that a strong body and mind go together: you can't improve one without working on the other. Have you ever noticed how you feel more alert after exercising? Training your body helps to clear your mind. It works the other way too: when your mind is focused, it's easier to master a new move.

Training teaches martial artists a lot about themselves – they get to know their strengths and weaknesses. It also teaches them about others, helping them to get along with different kinds of people. Each time you practice with a partner or size up an opponent, you get better at understanding how other people think and act.

All kinds of people in countries such as China, Japan, and Korea have studied martial arts – from monks and nuns, fishermen and farmers, to

The road less traveled

You might notice that the names of many martial arts end with the word *do* (doh) – tae kwon do, kendo, judo. Do means "path" or "way." It is the road the martial artist travels toward perfection and self-knowledge. In Asia, this path can be the martial arts or something else – painting or music, for instance.

Knowing other people is intelligence,
knowing yourself is wisdom.
Overcoming others takes strength,
overcoming yourself takes greatness.
    – *Lao-tzu*, Tao-te Ching

warriors and royalty. Many started training as kids, and they took a lifetime to perfect their skills.

It's only been in the past hundred years that people in the West have gotten to know the martial arts. With faster ways to travel, people and ideas now have an easier time moving around the globe. But why is there such interest in arts that started so long ago, in a faraway place? Life in one part of the world may be different than in another, but some ideas are exciting no matter who or where you are. The challenge to be your best – while having a lot of fun – has made the martial arts popular with kids and adults all over the world.

Beginnings

Where and how did the martial arts start?

In the story of the martial arts, it can be hard to separate the legends from the facts. The martial arts' origins are mysterious because for so long nothing was written down. What's more, techniques were often passed from master to student in secret.

We know that people have practiced fighting skills for thousands of years. Pictures on ancient tomb walls in Asia show what looks like people practicing martial arts, and legends tell of martial training in India. But the first true system of martial arts probably began in China during the AD 500s. The place was the Shaolin (sh-ow-lin) Temple, a Buddhist monastery hidden in the wilderness of Songshan mountain in Honan province.

The Story of Bodhidharma

It may come as a surprise that the first system of martial arts was designed to help monks sit still! Around the year AD 520, a monk from India called Bodhidharma (baw-dee-darma) traveled on foot to China. He wanted to share his new ideas with the monks at the Shaolin Temple. According to legend, Bodhidharma sat meditating – thinking quietly and deeply – in a cave outside the monastery for nine years after the head monk refused to let him in.

Finally, Bodhidharma's intense concentration pierced a hole in the cave wall, and the head monk was so amazed that he invited the visitor inside. There are many far-fetched stories about Bodhidharma, but we know that he did teach the monks his beliefs, which came to be known as Zen Buddhism. He told them they could reach the highest spiritual level – called enlightenment – if they emptied their minds of distracting thoughts and focused only on the present moment.

Today in Western countries we know the Shaolin martial arts as "kung fu." But in China this term means only "learned skill." It can describe any task a person has practiced and become good at – even knitting or playing chess! In China, *wushu* (woo-shoo) is the word for martial arts.

Bodhidharma was impressed by how devoted the Shaolin monks were to praying and studying scriptures, but he was surprised to see them in such weak physical shape. He thought a monk needed a strong body to use his mind to the fullest, and especially to sit still and meditate for a long time – without getting sore legs or falling asleep! And he believed that it was by meditating, not reading scriptures, that a monk gained true wisdom.

Bodhidharma got to work teaching the monks exercises to keep their bodies and minds strong. The first forms he taught them were called the Eighteen Hands of the Lo-han. These exercises, which later became known as kung fu, are the source for many of the different martial arts styles around today.

Under Bodhidharma's watchful eye, the monks trained their bodies and minds to be strong and disciplined.

The Five Animals

Learning from nature

The Shaolin monks soon began adding to Bodhidharma's exercises – and they didn't have to look far for ideas. Living in the mountains, they saw nature all around them every day. Legends tell of how they watched different animals and copied their movements, so they could gain each animal's special strengths for themselves. The monks chose five animals that had the most to teach them: the tiger, the leopard, the snake, the crane, and the dragon. The martial arts forms they named after these creatures are still used today.

Each animal stands for a feeling or an idea that the martial artist acts out as he practices the movements. Some forms are used for defense, others to attack.

The tiger and leopard are both powerful attack forms. When a tiger stalks its prey, it crouches low to the ground – then pounces with all its strength and speed. It uses both its claws and its strong legs to attack. In the same way, the martial artist who uses the tiger form keeps his body low and steady, and from this position makes powerful, fast strikes with his arms and legs. He might curve his fingers like the tiger's claws. The leopard is also known for its fast pounces and strength. This form makes good use of footwork and strategy.

The snake strikes its prey quickly, hitting a weak spot with deadly accuracy. Likewise, the snake form uses fast blows to vital areas to quickly stop an attacker.

The crane inspired a new form for self-defense. By standing on one leg like the bird, the martial artist learns excellent balance. From this stance she can defend herself with fast counterattacks. Her quick arm movements look like flapping wings, while high kicks and hops make her a hard target to attack.

The Shaolin monks even tried to imagine how the mythical dragon would fight, so they could learn something from this powerful animal too. The dragon style uses a series of fast, forceful attacks that don't let up. Martial masters believe this form

Monkeying around

While the Five Animals are basic to Chinese martial arts, other animals have inspired martial artists as well. And some of them seem like strange choices at first!

The Drunken Monkey style imitates the weaving movements of monkeys who have eaten spoiled fruit. The martial artist who uses this style looks like an easy target – off balance and stumbling about. But appearances are deceiving: he is actually solid on his feet and ready to strike with a quick counterattack if needed. His opponent may underestimate him and let down his guard. This style is fun to watch but hard to learn. Only highly trained martial artists try this form.

strengthens a person's inner spirit – it is the sign of an advanced martial artist.

There is another story of how animal movements inspired the martial arts. Hua To was a famous doctor who lived long before Bodhidharma, in the AD 200s. He invented exercises that imitated five animals: the tiger, the bear, the bird, the deer, and the monkey. Hua To believed his exercises would make people healthy. Over time martial artists began to use his ideas to improve their own skills.

The Art of Self-Defense

At first the monks used Bodhidharma's exercises to stay strong and alert. But as they traveled between monasteries to share teachings, they often met with bandits on China's dangerous roads. And their own temple was in the wilderness – a prime target for gangs of thieves. Soon they began to use their new strength to defend themselves.

Stories of the monks' talents spread far and wide, and the emperor asked for their help to fight off invading enemies. Shaolin martial arts became famous, and more people came to the temple to learn from these experts. The monks' bravery in good causes inspired many legends about them. These tales sometimes exaggerated their skills, making them sound invincible or superhuman.

Although there are many myths about Shaolin martial artists, one thing seems certain: the monks used their special skills only for self-defense or to defend their temple or country. Even so, their ideal was to avoid fighting altogether. A Shaolin monk's training gave him two special skills: a sharp mind and self-control. He used the first to avoid danger and the second to solve a problem without losing his temper. Today's martial artists still share this belief, and would rather use their heads than their hands to protect themselves.

Fighting without using hands

An old story about a Japanese samurai (warrior)
shows how true martial artists treat fighting as
a last resort, and prefer to use strategy to end a conflict.

A samurai named Tsukahara Bokuden was once traveling on a ferry boat full of people. Also on board was another samurai who was drunk and pushing the passengers around. When he saw Bokuden sitting quietly, he challenged him to a fight to prove how tough he was.

Bokuden knew that any fighting between them could hurt one of the passengers, so he answered, "My style of fighting is very advanced – I don't use my sword or my hands." The drunken man thought this was some kind of insult, and demanded they begin right away.

Bokuden shook his head, saying, "We can't fight here – there are too many people on this boat. Let's go over to that small island instead."

The other samurai agreed, and the boat's captain steered them to the island. Beside himself with anger, the challenger jumped off the boat onto the shore and turned to face his opponent, his sword raised. But Bokuden stayed on the boat. As he quickly pushed it out to sea with an oar, he called, "That is the way of fighting without using hands!"

To win one hundred battles in one hundred wars is not the ultimate skill. To stop the enemy without fighting is the ultimate skill.
– Sun Tzu, The Art of War

The Spiritual Side of the Martial Arts

It can be hard at first to see what's so spiritual about the martial arts. When you watch the punches and kicks, it seems to be all about a strong, fast body. But there's more happening than that. You may not be able to see the spiritual side, but it's there, under the surface.

Martial artists have always known that training your body without working on your mind too is a waste of time. If you don't concentrate, your movements are just jabs in the air. And whether you're getting ready to train or to face an opponent, one of the best ways to focus your mind is meditation.

A martial artist trains to be the best person he can be – in body and mind – but he also knows he is part of a community and, beyond that, of the natural world. He knows how important it is to help others and to live in harmony with nature. Keeping all these goals in mind can get complicated, so martial artists have looked for help from philosophies – ways of thinking, acting, and understanding the world.

Zen Buddhism, Taoism, and Confucianism are three philosophies that have always played a key role in the martial arts. They give the martial artist a code to follow, showing her how to use her skills for good, not for hurting others. And they help keep her on the path to becoming her best, in mind and body.

In Japan, people have long practiced special arts to help them understand the ways of Zen. Besides the martial arts, these "Zen arts" include archery, flower arrangement, and the tea ceremony.

Zen Buddhism

The here and now

Bodhidharma's teachings started a new kind of Buddhism – what the Japanese call Zen, and what is known in China as Chan. Zen shaped the way many people think about and practice the martial arts, from Chinese monks to Japanese warriors to today's martial arts students. And at the heart of Zen is meditation.

Who was Buddha?

The name "Buddha" means "enlightened one" and was given to honor the founder of Buddhism, Siddhartha Gautama. Legends and facts are mixed up in what we know of Buddha's life. Gautama was probably born in the 500s BC near the Himalayas. The son of rich parents, he led a carefree life. But one day he ventured out of his palace and saw people suffering. Then he came across a monk begging for food and felt he had seen his destiny. He could never return to the luxury of his old life.

He wandered in search of truth, and after years of looking without success, he sat down quietly under a tree. There he finally reached enlightenment. From that moment he began to preach his new beliefs.

Got a lot on your mind? Maybe too much at times? In Zen meditation, a person's mind is like a cup being turned over. The goal is to empty it of all thoughts. Now you're free to feel only the present moment. With no worries to distract you, you can see things more clearly. You can also react quickly to anything that happens – including an attack by an opponent. Today, many martial arts classes still begin or end with students sitting, eyes closed, in meditation.

For Zen Buddhists, the goal of all this meditating is to reach enlightenment. This experience is hard to describe, but some Zen teachers call it a sudden flash in your mind, when illusions disappear and you can "see" the true nature of the universe and your place in it.

The Shaolin monks' exercises not only helped them meditate but also made their bodies strong enough to

When you seek it, you cannot find it …
When you no longer seek it,
it is always with you.
– Zen proverb

Scientists know that meditation can make people feel better and worry less. Besides helping you relax, it also has a good effect on the parts of your body that you can't control by thinking about them – blood pressure and digestion, for instance. Studies have also shown that meditating can ease pain and help the body fight disease. Scientists are still trying to understand why it works in these ways.

handle enlightenment – which could be an overwhelming experience! Their martial arts could even help them reach enlightenment more quickly. Hundreds of years later, the Zen master Hakuin described the power of training the mind and body together. He claimed that a month of martial arts was worth a whole year of sitting still to meditate.

Zen was different from traditional Buddhism. Zen followers didn't study scriptures – they focused on the here and now. They believed that wisdom should be passed from mind to mind, with few words and without writing things down. In fact, one of Zen's greatest teachers, Hui-neng, who lived in the AD 600s, could neither read nor write. Zen masters taught their disciples with riddles, questions, and stories. These conversations were used to snap students out of their usual ways of thinking.

Two of Buddhism's great rules also shaped the early martial arts. The first was to avoid harming any living creature. The second was tolerance – to accept other people as they are. For the martial artist this meant avoiding violence whenever possible, and living in harmony with others.

Taoism

The way and its power

Around 2,500 years ago, a man named Lao-tzu (loud-zoo) rode toward the western border of China. He was saddened by the evil ways of so many people and wanted to spend the last years of his life in the peace of the wilderness. A border guard recognized the traveler and asked him to leave a record of his teachings. Lao-tzu agreed and stopped to write a collection of short, mysterious poems. These simple but wise words – about life, the universe, and our place in it – came to be known as the *Tao-te Ching* (dow dah jing), "The Way and Its Power."

We don't know for sure how much of this legend is true, but no matter how the *Tao-te Ching* was written, it came to play an important role in Chinese society and ideas – and in the martial arts.

The Tao – which means "way" – is really two things. It is the path that nature follows in its cycles – day and night, summer and winter. But it is also the source of everything in the world, something without a name that we can never fully know. The philosophy that grew from these ideas is called Taoism (dow-ism), which means "following the way."

Lao-tzu warned that following the way wasn't easy. But he left clues about how to try. People would be happier if they led simple lives – taking things as they are and letting go of

Stiff and unbending is the principle of death.
Gentle and yielding is the principle of life.
So an army without flexibility never wins a battle.
A tree that is unbending is easily broken.
The hard and strong will fall.
The soft and weak will overcome.
– Lao-tzu, Tao-te Ching

selfish wants. Violence solves nothing, and ends up hurting the person who uses it. It is much better to be soft and flexible than strong and hard, trying to resist change.

Another key idea in Taoism – and for the martial arts – is "ch'i" (chee), known as "ki" in Japan. This word has many meanings, but basically it describes the energy in all living things. It is strong in newborn babies

Confucius

The teachings of Confucius – who lived about the same time as Lao-tzu – also shaped how people thought about the martial arts. Confucius lived during an age of war, but he believed in a well-ordered society, with just rulers and people who acted responsible for one another. Together with Taoism and Zen, Confucianism helped guide martial artists on their path of learning and training.

and weaker in people who are sick. Tapping into the power of ch'i is an important goal for the martial artist. Traditional Chinese medicine teaches that the center of this life force is found in your lower stomach, just below your navel (but you can't see it!). Breathing and moving in special ways can make the most of the ch'i that's there, and direct it through your body to where it is needed most – to power a strike or to heal an injury.

Yin and yang

You may have heard the saying "opposites attract." Taoism teaches that they go hand in hand.

At the heart of Taoism is the symbol of yin and yang (known as in-yo in Japan). All opposites – dark and light, female and male – balance each other. Each one needs the other to be complete. This balance is shown by the small light circle in the dark half and the small dark circle in the light half.

You can see yin and yang at work everywhere – in nature, in the way people get along, and in the martial arts. Strength and power are not enough if you don't know when to back down. The names of some martial arts forms show this balance of opposites. "Grasping the sparrow's tail while warding off the tiger" is a movement in the martial art of tai chi. Its name describes how softness and strength work in harmony.

Healing Arts

The hand that takes life also gives it

Along with Zen and the martial arts, Buddhists who traveled from India to China also brought new ideas about medicine. One of these was the belief that four elements of nature – earth, fire, water, and wind – control our bodies. In a healthy person these elements are balanced, while too much of any one can make you sick.

This notion took hold in many schools of martial arts. Each element stood for a special quality the martial artist should have. Fire is fast and bold – good traits for a martial artist. But water, soft and flowing, can put out fire. And so, balance is the key. Working on one quality while ignoring the others will make you a weak martial artist.

Martial arts and Chinese medicine have other ideas in common too. They both connect a healthy body with a healthy spirit. What's more, martial masters have a special knowledge of the human body and how it works. They know the body's vital areas – where a strike or arm-lock can stop an opponent. This know-how can also be used to heal, and in the past many schools of martial arts were also medical clinics. A common saying pointed out that "the hand that takes life also gives it."

When a master used his skills to heal, he put the philosophy behind his martial art into action. His training was not only good for himself but for others as well.

The power to heal

In the early days of judo, the students at one judo school heard about a gang of robbers who were troubling their town. One night the students snuck out into the dark streets, and they soon caught the robbers in the act. The thieves turned on them and the students were forced to defend themselves. The fight that followed was short, with the robbers quickly defeated. Wounded, the thieves retreated into the night.

The next day the judo students were surprised to see the same robbers show up at their school – which was also a clinic – to have their injuries treated. The robbers did not recognize the men they had fought in the dark the night before. And the judo experts tried not to smile as they bandaged the robbers, all the while noticing how effective their martial arts had been!

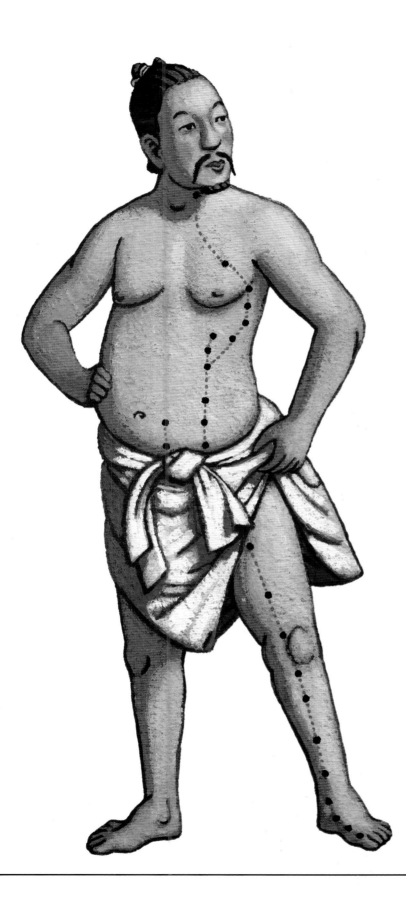

On pins and needles: acupuncture and ch'i

What do the martial arts and sticking pins have in common? Ch'i, of course!

One of Chinese medicine's best known treatments is acupuncture, a practice that's been around for thousands of years. It is based on the idea that ch'i (a person's life force) moves through the body along channels – a lot like a system of rivers. Ch'i isn't blood, but it is connected to it. You can't see or touch ch'i, but you can see the effect it has on someone. It makes a healthy person feel good and full of life. Some martial artists have described ch'i as a heat or energy flowing through them as they train. But when you don't have much ch'i or it is unbalanced, you'll feel sick or tired.

People who practice acupuncture believe you can control the flow of ch'i at special points along its channels. To do this they stick a very fine needle in at the right place. Or they sometimes use pressure, heat, electricity, or even lasers at the special points. Needles might be used to increase the flow of ch'i to an injured leg to speed up healing, or to direct ch'i to certain organs to treat a disease.

The goal is to keep the body balanced – so that blood, fluid, and ch'i all move as they should.

Many Branches, One Tree

The different styles of martial art

So how did there get to be so many kinds of martial art? All the names can get confusing, but each one grew from the same source.

After the Shaolin monks began sharing their martial arts with others, their techniques were changed over time, as students became masters and passed on what they had learned. How the new martial artists used their skills depended on where they lived and who they were.

For instance, fishermen might come to practice the martial arts rather differently than people who lived high in the mountains. While the sailors would need to keep their legs steady on rocking boats, the mountain climbers could use their strong legs for kicks. The threats people faced also changed their self-defense methods. They might be conquered by a foreign army and have to train in secret, or they might seek ways to fend off pirates and bandits. And the way they thought about themselves and the world shaped their martial arts, too – whether they were Buddhists, Taoists, or followers of Confucius.

Shaolin Temple Boxing

The original kung fu

China has many martial arts styles, but they all fall into one of two groups – either "hard, external" or "soft, internal." Hard styles meet force with force. They're called external because this force moves out from a person with fast, powerful strikes by the arms and legs. On the other hand, soft styles use dodges and throws to avoid an attack. Instead of fast blocks and jabs, these martial arts feature circular movements that flow smoothly from one to the next.

Shaolin Temple boxing – what many people know as kung fu – is the most famous of China's hard, external styles. Shaolin boxers use direct thrusts with their hands or feet, making the most of their physical power. Training toughens their bodies and makes them stronger.

Over time, Bodhidharma's exercises for the Shaolin monks started to change in different parts of China. People in the north, who lived in the mountains, were generally bigger and had strong legs from walking uphill on bumpy ground. So they used their height and legs to advantage, with large movements and jumping kicks. Meanwhile, China's southerners were mostly farmers with smaller builds who worked with their hands. They made use of their strong hands and arms in their moves, and kept their feet planted more firmly on the ground.

Today, kids from across China travel to the rebuilt Shaolin Temple to study martial arts. High in the mountains, students from the age of 6 to 18 train in wushu – as well as the more usual school subjects. When they graduate, some might become health workers or open their own martial arts schools – while a few will stay on to become Buddhist monks or nuns.

Tai Chi Chuan

The soft art of Taoism

Each morning across China, people can be seen on rooftops and in parks, moving their arms and legs in slow, graceful patterns. They are practicing the most famous "soft, internal" martial art – tai chi chuan (tie chee choo-wan). Tai chi's flowing movements are believed to clear your mind, make you healthier, and even help you to live longer.

At first glance tai chi may not look like a martial art at all. There are no fast kicks or strikes as in Shaolin Temple boxing. That's because tai chi – and other soft arts such as chi kung and pa kua – is about building your inner strength.

Tai chi is practiced by young and old – over 100 million people around the world. Its gentle movements are believed to help people recover from sickness or injury.

Students learn to breathe in a way that increases the life force called "ch'i" in their bodies. As they move slowly through a series of forms, they keep their minds focused and their bodies relaxed and balanced.

From the outside their bodies might look soft, but inside there is a core of strength. One tai chi master, Ch'en Wei-ming, described the arms of a person doing tai chi as "iron wrapped in cotton." Here is the Taoist idea of yin-yang in action – the opposites of strength and flexibility in perfect balance.

Most people do not study tai chi for self-defense, but its moves can be used this way by a master. Instead of blocking one attack with another, the tai chi expert gives way to the attack, turning the opponent's energy to her own advantage. The attacker's blow meets no resistance – and with nothing solid to lay hold of, the blow can do no harm. Tai chi masters have been known to defeat stronger, larger opponents who use a hard style.

In China, tai chi is one of the five skills believed to make you a better person. The others are painting, poetry, calligraphy, and music.

Family tai

The Yang family of China were famous tai chi teachers who lived in the 1800s. Many legends are told about their amazing skills.

Yang Lu-ch'uan was once challenged to a contest by a young Chinese boxer who wanted to prove himself against the famous tai chi master. When the challenger landed a forceful blow on his stomach, Lu-ch'uan let out his breath in a laugh – one that knocked the boxer nine meters (30 feet) across the room!

Lu-ch'uan's son Yang Chien-hou was said to be able to keep a swallow on the palm of his hand. Every time the bird tried to escape, Chien-hou would yield a little with his hand, and the bird had no solid base from which to take off.

Nothing is softer or more yielding than water, but when it attacks things hard and resistant, not one of them can prevail … That the yielding conquers the resistant and the soft conquers the hard is a fact known by all, yet used by no one.
– *Lao-tzu*, Tao-te Ching

Twisting snake, swooping hawk

Tai chi is one of the oldest martial arts. Its origins are a mystery, and little was written about it until around 1750. It might be based on Chinese breathing exercises invented over 2,000 years ago. But the most popular theory about tai chi's beginnings is the story of Chang San-feng, a Taoist priest who lived in the 1400s.

One day outside his mountain home, Chang San-feng saw a hawk attack a snake. He watched the snake defend itself by backing up and twisting this way and that. The hawk's sharp beak and talons were useless as the snake coiled and circled. Suddenly San-feng realized that a weaker person could defeat a stronger one by yielding in clever ways. He invented exercises based on this idea – but his aim was to make people healthier and wiser, not better fighters.

Karate

The empty hand

China's monks also traveled outside their country, and they took their martial arts skills with them. One of the places where they left their mark was the island of Okinawa (now part of Japan). There, fishermen and farmers learned Shaolin techniques from Chinese travelers, and they used them to defend themselves against the pirates who troubled their island.

Weapons were outlawed in Okinawa in 1480 by King Sho Shin, a Buddhist who rejected violence. And when the Japanese conquered Okinawa in 1609, they made it illegal for the islanders to practice any martial arts – only Japanese warriors could do that. Secretly, the Okinawans kept training.

The system they had learned from the Chinese became known as "karate," and it gave the conquered Okinawans a way to stay strong and protect themselves.

Karate students – then and now – practice *kata*, a series of attack and defense movements that is like a living dictionary of karate techniques. To the Japanese invaders, *kata* looked like traditional dances, which helped the Okinawans to keep karate a secret.

Students start off with simple postures, such as the "horse-riding" stance. Holding this position makes their legs strong and gives them a stable base from which to strike with their arms. In traditional training, it could take up to two years to master the basics before moving on to advanced techniques.

Get a grip

In some karate styles – such as Goju-Ryu – students used special exercises to make their grip more powerful. Kanshu, or "penetration hand," was one they learned from the Chinese. A student would push his hand into a jar filled with powder. Once this became too easy, he switched to a jar filled with rice, then sand, then beans, and finally pebbles. In another exercise, students carried a jar by its mouth with their fingers. At first the jar was empty, but then it was filled with more and more water.

Students of karate often let out a loud yell when they strike with their hand or kick. The sound they make, "kiai" (key-eye), is known as the "spirit shout" in Japanese. It is used to focus all of your ch'i – or "ki" in Japan – at a target.

In time, karate changed and started to look different from the Chinese art it grew from. It does not use the Chinese animal forms, and has kept only a few of the monks' circular moves during stepping, turning, and blocking. In karate, your body's weight is often shared evenly between your two feet – some say because Okinawa's fishermen needed to be stable on their boats. And while Chinese wushu styles use light, flowing movements to avoid an attack, karate's style is harder and more direct – more like a straight line than a circle. It is known for the straight thrust of a closed fist.

On average, people in Okinawa live longer than anywhere else in the world. Doctors and scientists have studied why Okinawans live so long and are so healthy. One reason is the way they make martial arts part of daily life. This not only makes them fit but also keeps them in touch with their spiritual beliefs.

What's in a name?

The Okinawans named their martial art "karate," which means "China-hand," to honor the Chinese travelers who brought it to their island. But the character for "China" was later changed to mean "empty," showing that this was an art without weapons – the art of the empty hand.

Karate is "empty" in other ways too. The great karate master Gichin Funakoshi described how the karate student must empty himself of selfishness and evil, and become like a polished mirror that reflects what is around him. Like the Zen monks, he can then react in the best way to whatever happens – whether it's an attack, an emergency, or a tough situation.

When your hand goes out, withdraw your anger. When your anger goes out, withdraw your hand. – Okinawan proverb

Tae Kwon Do

Korea's martial art

Travelers heading east from China soon brought the Shaolin martial arts to the shores of Korea. There, people used them to defend the coast against pirates and other enemies. The first name the Koreans gave this empty-hand style was t'ang-su – which means "T'ang hand." They named it after the T'ang royal family (AD 618–907), who ruled China at the time. You can still spot over fifty circular Chinese hand movements in modern tae kwon do (tay-kwawn-doh).

Because Korea lies between China and Japan, it has often been a meeting place for the two cultures. So it's no surprise that today's tae kwon do looks a little like both Chinese and Japanese martial arts. When the Japanese invaded Korea in the 1500s, they introduced arts such as ju-jitsu. In the early 1900s, Japan invaded Korea again, and this time they brought their ideas about training school-age kids in judo and kendo. After Japan was defeated at the end of the Second World War, in 1945, Korea was once again in control of its martial arts. In the 1950s, South Korea's different martial arts schools united into one system under the name *tae kwon do*.

Today's tae kwon do uses both the quick, straight movements of karate and the flowing, circular moves of

wushu. It is also known for its high, jumping kicks. The way tae kwon do uses the whole body is shown by its name, "the way of the foot and fist." Like other "do" forms, it is more than a system of moves. It is a way of living and thinking, of always trying to be your best – in mind, body, and character.

Tae kwon do has been around since the 1950s, but its story – under different names – is much older. Today, people in more than 140 countries practice tae kwon do, and it became an official Olympic sport in 2000. Competitors protect themselves with headgear and padding when they face an opponent.

Hwarang-do: the young warrior's code

For hundreds of years, Korea was divided into three kingdoms – Koguryo, Paekche, and Silla. During the 600s, Silla's Queen Songdok sent young students to China to study martial arts. She also started a school where the sons of noble families could learn martial arts and philosophy. Boys between the ages of 16 and 20 went there to learn about Buddhism, the teachings of Confucius, and the military strategy of the writer Sun Tzu. They trained in the empty-hand martial art known as subak – later to become tae kwon do – and learned to fight with swords, use a bow and arrow, and ride horses.

In time this school grew into a way of life called hwarang-do (h-wah-rung-doh), which means "the way of flowering man-hood." The boys lived by a code that was based on five rules: be loyal and trust-worthy, respect your parents, and show courage and fairness. The goal of Queen Songdok's training was to turn these boys into the best-educated men of their class – as well as the best warriors.

Weapons in Martial Arts

You may have seen martial artists sparring not only with their hands and feet but with a sword or staff as well. So where do weapons like these fit into the martial arts? The armed martial arts have a different story than the arts of the "empty hand." But the two stories are connected, and each has shaped the other.

Peasants in Okinawa sometimes used their farm tools for self-defense. The kama (on the left) was originally a sickle for harvesting rice. The tonfa (peasant in the center) was the handle of a rice grinder, while the nunchaku (on the right) was a flail for threshing rice.

In China, the Shaolin monks couldn't use weapons as these were forbidden by the teachings of Buddhism. Their martial arts were empty-handed from the start, and very different from the skills of Chinese warriors. These soldiers used weapons but did not have a very high place in Chinese society.

Over time the Shaolin monks started to use religious objects, such as the priest's staff, to defend themselves when they needed to. And warriors began to train in the unarmed martial arts, adding these new techniques to their skills with weapons.

Today in China, martial arts students usually learn empty-hand

skills first. After years of practice they might add weapons to their training. Wushu weapons come from two very old sources. There are those the warrior carried – the sword or the spear. But other weapons come from somewhere you might not expect: the farm! Ordinary people used farm tools such as the pitchfork or hoe for self-defense, not only in China but in Okinawa as well.

In Japan, weapons have a very different story. The Japanese warrior – the samurai – was honored, and so armed martial arts were well respected. Warrior schools taught weapons skills first, followed by empty-hand techniques. Weapons such as the sword have long been important symbols in Japan.

The Samurai

The way of the warrior

The Japanese warrior was an awesome sight. Riding into battle on horseback, covered in splendid armor and armed with two curved swords, he knew how to face danger without flinching. He may have lived in a long-ago age, but his ideas and way of life have stayed at the heart of today's martial arts in Japan.

These warriors were known as *samurai* (sa-moo-reye), a name that means "to serve." They started out as hired men who protected rich landowners. But by the 1100s they had become powerful themselves. Japanese society was divided into strict classes, where everyone knew his place – and the samurai were lucky enough to be near the very top. They had many special rights: they could carry swords, judge court cases, and take human life – including their own if they faced disgrace. But in return they followed a strict code, known as *bushido* (boo-shee-doh), "the way of the warrior." To be true to bushido, the samurai had to be completely loyal to his lord and use his skills with self-control and mercy. In many ways bushido was like the European knight's code of chivalry during the Middle Ages.

When a boy in a samurai family turned five, he was given an imitation sword in a special ceremony. He carried this symbol of his rank and duties from then on, and began to prepare for the samurai life. He learned empty-hand martial arts but made the most of his right to carry weapons and ride a horse. At martial arts schools called "ryu" he trained in sword fighting – kenjutsu (the art of the drawn sword) and iaijutsu (the art of drawing the sword). Samurai schools also taught strategy – including how to avoid a fight altogether by using your head.

> Samurai women and girls trained with weapons too. The samurai's wife and daughters learned to use the naginata, a long pole with a blade on one end. With it they defended the family home and honor while the samurai was away.

EMPEROR: Japan's "divine" ruler. Believed to be descended from the gods, he protects Japan's religious and cultural traditions.

The world of the samurai

When warriors ruled Japan, everyone was born into a class – and stayed there. This strict system took shape from the 1100s on, and was firmly in place by the time of the Tokugawa shoguns, or Edo Period – which lasted over 250 years, from the early 1600s to the mid-1800s.

SHOGUN: The strongest warrior in the country, he rules Japan in the name of the emperor.

DAIMYO (die-myoh): Local warlords who rule their lands from a castle-town. They serve the shogun and collect taxes from local villages and farms.

SAMURAI: Warriors who serve the daimyo. When not fighting, they busy themselves with training and studying Zen. (The shogun and daimyo also belong to the samurai class.)

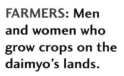

FARMERS: Men and women who grow crops on the daimyo's lands.

ARTISANS: Potters, tailors, and all those who make things that others need.

Other people with special roles belonged to groups outside the class system – such as priests and nuns, doctors, teachers, and entertainers.

"NON-HUMANS": Outcasts who do dirty jobs others would rather not think about – such as cleaning garbage off the streets.

MERCHANTS: People who buy and sell goods. They are in a lower class than farmers and artisans because they produce nothing of their own.

Here today, gone tomorrow

Japanese poets have often compared the life of the samurai to the cherry blossom. In Japan the cherry tree is prized for its beautiful flowers, which bloom for a short while in spring but disappear suddenly with a strong wind or rainstorm. In the same way, the samurai's life was glorious but brief. At any time he could be called upon to die for his cause.

To face this fate bravely, the samurai turned to Zen Buddhism. Zen meditation emptied his mind of distractions, so he could react to the enemy he faced without worrying about anything else. Zen also taught him not to become too attached to life, and to live as if each moment were his last.

The best fate the samurai hoped for was to die in battle or while defending his lord, or "daimyo." About the worst thing that could happen was for his daimyo to die before him. Without a master, the samurai became known as a "ronin" (roh-nin). This was shameful because people might think he had failed to protect his daimyo, or else had behaved badly and been sent away. Some ronin became martial arts teachers or bodyguards for people in lower classes.

For hundreds of years – from the 1000s to the 1600s – Japan was torn apart by wars among its powerful clans, each with its own samurai and army. The samurai way of life continued well into the 1800s, since Japan's class system stayed much the same during peace and war. But as Japan began to have more contact with Western countries, it started using modern ideas about governments and armies. This meant doing away with the old classes, and taking power from the shogun and putting it back into the hands of the emperor and his government. The samurai lost many of their privileges, including their right to carry swords and to wear their hair in the traditional topknot.

Too proud to accept this fate, the samurai made one last stand in 1877. At the Satsuma rebellion, 40,000 samurai with traditional weapons faced a modern army with firepower. Amazingly, even with the odds so heavily against them, the samurai fought for seven months before being defeated! In the end the rebellion's leader took his own life on the battlefield, and the samurai were forced to accept the new era.

Today in Japan, only sumo wrestlers have the privilege to wear their hair in the samurai topknot that once symbolized the warrior class. This hairstyle shows the sumo's samurai rank and must be removed if he leaves his profession.

Ninjas

The art of being invisible

While Japan's samurai rode proudly into battle, another kind of martial artist acted in the shadows. They were the ninjas, whose name means "someone who steals in." These highly trained spies were feared but not well respected. Unlike the samurai, who faced their opponents openly, ninjas worked slyly behind the scenes to trick the enemy.

For centuries Japan's powerful clans fought one another, and they hired ninjas for all sorts of missions: spying, sabotage, or spreading false information to confuse the enemy. Samurai often hired them to do the jobs they felt were too dirty for a warrior, but ninjas worked for other people too. One prince who was famous for making just rulings on court cases had his ninja spies to thank for his wisdom. They researched both sides of the case to find out who was lying!

The shuriken, or throwing star, was a round piece of metal with sharp blades. It was often used by a cornered ninja – who could use it to hit a target up to 11 meters (35 feet) away.

Tricks of the trade

Ninjas were always coming up with new tricks to fool their enemies and move among them unnoticed. A ninja disguised as a priest might pretend to be sick outside an enemy stronghold so he would be taken inside.

On many missions, a ninja had to sneak around inside enemy homes at night – a tough job, since guards often slept on floors throughout the house. Ninjas were trained to know the difference between someone who was really asleep and someone who was pretending, by listening to their snoring and the tiny sounds made by moving joints. They would step over a person sleeping soundly, but a faker wouldn't be so lucky!

Ninjas were also careful to cover their tracks so they couldn't be followed. They were good at "sideways walking" – with feet facing in opposite directions so their footprints didn't show which way they were heading.

So how did someone get to be a ninja? It ran in the family. Ninja families lived together in wild mountain areas, where they could train in secret. In well-guarded villages they created their martial art of ninjitsu – a blend of empty-hand self-defense, weapons, escape techniques, and disguises. Dressed up as a priest, actor, or farmer, a ninja looked harmless enough to get close to the enemy. Ninjas also learned to dance, sing, and practice different trades to make their disguises convincing.

Training was tough, and it started young. Both girls and boys began when they were five or six years old. They walked on narrow logs to improve their balance and hung from trees by their hands to strengthen their arms. Each day, they ran, swam, and climbed for hours to make their bodies strong and flexible. By the age of twelve or thirteen they were training with weapons such as swords, spears, or staffs. And they learned to throw the ninja's favorite weapon, the shuriken, or throwing star.

Ninjas on the move traveled light. They carried everything they needed for a mission and dressed to blend in with their surroundings. Brown clothes worked best for night missions inside an enemy's house. Ninjas hid small weapons and tools in the folds of their clothes, such as a tiny bow and arrow or a rope ladder for climbing castle

Masters of escape

Like many martial artists, ninjas looked to nature for inspiration. They based their favorite means of escape on five natural elements: water, fire, wood, metal, and earth. Wood stood for climbing a tree and blending in with the leaves. Starting a fire could distract guards, giving the ninja a chance to sneak away. Earth held ways to blend in with the landscape – by rolling up into a ball to look like a stone, the ninja could lie unseen. Metal came in handy in the small blades the ninja threw to create a diversion. And water was a very useful means of escape. A ninja might float away, hidden in a pile of weeds he had thrown on the surface of a stream.

Girl ninjas were known as "Deadly Flowers." They often snuck into enemy homes disguised as dancers or servants in order to spy.

walls. Each weapon or tool could be used for more than one job. Throwing stars were good for self-defense or for digging, and the scabbard that held a sword doubled as a snorkel – handy for hiding underwater.

In peacetime Japan there was less demand for the ninjas' skills. Sometimes they worked as bodyguards or did jobs for the police. But many ninjitsu skills did not survive modern technology very well; electricity makes it hard to hide in dark corners! Today some martial arts masters are working to re-create ninjitsu as a more positive style of self-defense.

The last ninja? Seiko Fujita (1899–1966)

Many people believe that Seiko Fujita – who took on missions for Japan's imperial government – was the last practicing ninja. His grandfather trained him in ninjitsu, and Fujita went to extremes to teach himself to ignore pain and survive poison. He stuck needles in his skin. He ate rat poison, wall lizards, glass, and even brick. He recalled that the glass was easy but the brick took him 40 minutes!

Fujita claimed to be the last ninja and said the secrets of ninjitsu would die with him. He had no patience for the ninja fad that was popular with Japanese teenagers in the 1960s, and was sorry to see ninjitsu being used to sell everything from comic books to movies.

Kendo

The way of the sword

The samurai perfected his sword fighting over a lifetime of practice. But how could samurai train without hurting each other, sometimes fatally? And during peacetime, with no enemy to fight on the battlefield, samurai still wanted to sharpen their skills with contests. How could they avoid injuries? The answer was to use a wooden or bamboo sword for practice. And once real swords were made illegal in Japan in 1876, this became the only way to keep the art of the sword alive.

From the samurai art of kenjutsu grew the martial art of kendo – "the way of the sword." But instead of preparing you for combat, kendo offered a way to get all the benefits of training without the risk of fatal sword contests. At first some samurai looked down on the new art. They thought it was a show that ronin – samurai without masters – put on to make a living. But serious kendo artists had higher ideals. They knew that the discipline needed for kendo was a way to improve your mind, body, and spirit together.

In modern kendo, skill and technique are more important than size and strength. That makes it a martial art that kids, women, and men of all different sizes can do. The kendo uniform protects your head and body, and rules limit which body parts can be targets: the head, the side of the body, the throat, and the wrists. Students, called kendoka, use a wooden sword to practice the exercises known as "kata" in pairs. For matches they use the shinai, a mock sword made of split bamboo wrapped in leather. Ritual and

> Bladed weapons have long been a special part of Japan's culture, and the hoko (a kind of lance) is the oldest one, even older than the sword. A story from Japanese mythology tells of how the god Izanagi created Japan. Standing on the Bridge of Heaven, he thrust his hoko into the ocean below. As he lifted it out, he shook off the drops of water, which fell into the sea and formed the islands of Japan.

The sword is the soul of a warrior ... when you draw a sword you are holding your soul in your hands.
– Morihei Ueshiba, founder of aikido

The kendo uniform recalls the samurai of the past. The hakama, a split skirt, has seven pleats that stand for the seven Confucian virtues of the warrior: kindness, honor, courtesy, wisdom, sincerity, loyalty, and piety. It is tied with a knot near the lower stomach, the source of the energy called ki (or "ch'i" in China).

discipline are important in kendo. It may be the least practical of the martial arts – you're not likely to use kendo for self-defense on the street! But that is not the purpose of kendo.

Today, kendo is one of the most respected martial arts in Japan. Kendoka believe their training helps them to become more positive, self-confident, and mature – and teaches them to react quickly to unexpected events. That might be why kendo is popular with so many kinds of people – from the Japanese police to Japanese kids.

From Temple to Training Hall

The martial arts move into the modern age

The martial arts gave all sorts of people – monks, farmers, fishermen – a way to stay strong and alert, and to defend themselves. This made some governments nervous. They thought the martial arts were dangerous – especially in the hands of people they had conquered. Afraid of rebellions, some rulers banned the martial arts. Training became a secret practice often done at night.

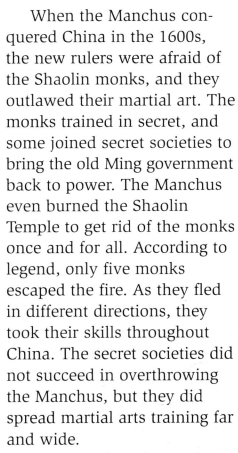

When the Manchus conquered China in the 1600s, the new rulers were afraid of the Shaolin monks, and they outlawed their martial art. The monks trained in secret, and some joined secret societies to bring the old Ming government back to power. The Manchus even burned the Shaolin Temple to get rid of the monks once and for all. According to legend, only five monks escaped the fire. As they fled in different directions, they took their skills throughout China. The secret societies did not succeed in overthrowing the Manchus, but they did spread martial arts training far and wide.

Karate and tae kwon do were also forbidden for a time. When Okinawa and Korea were conquered by Japan, training was outlawed. But masters continued to pass on their skills to disciples in secret.

In fact, many martial artists got so used to their secret ways that they continued them even after the bans ended.

Master and Disciple

A boy knocks on the door of the martial arts school near his village in China. He has brought a gift to show his respect, and hopes to convince the master to take him on as a student. He knows that even if he succeeds, he will be handed over to a senior student for a time to learn the basics. His training will be long and tiring. At times he won't even see what it has to do with learning martial arts! Like many others before him, he might give up and go home.

But if he sticks it out, his discipline will pay off. The master is watching him and will decide when he is ready to move on to bigger things. After many years he may even become one of the master's trusted disciples, and learn the most advanced forms of his martial art.

The traditional give-and-take between master and disciple was full of rituals and rules. It was very different from how we think about students and teachers today in the West.

Once the martial arts were legal again, many masters opened schools, but they continued to keep much of their art secret, for a few reasons. For one, Zen teaches never to tell anything too plainly – it's better for a student to wonder and think about a new truth. Some teachers believed that sharing knowledge bit by bit would make it seem more valuable to their students.

And masters knew that advanced techniques could be deadly in the wrong hands. They waited for a worthy student to take their place, and saved the most advanced moves for that special person. If the right disciple never came along, the technique could die with the master.

A student's early training might include hard, boring tasks – such as filling and carrying water buckets – to teach discipline.

The Founder of Modern Karate

When Funakoshi wanted to test himself, he turned to nature rather than a human opponent. He would stay outside during fierce storms, holding his stance against strong winds.

One person deserves much of the credit for bringing karate from Okinawa to Japan – and from there to the world. But this karate master wasn't a born athlete or leader. He started out as a shy, weak kid.

Born in Okinawa in 1870, Gichin Funakoshi was small and frail as a child, with little self-confidence. This began to change when he met the father of one of his classmates – a karate master.

The Japanese had banned karate in Okinawa, so Funakoshi trained in secret in his master's backyard at night. Over time he became healthier and more confident. When he grew up, Funakoshi himself secretly taught karate. Once it was made legal, Funakoshi became a respected master who could teach openly.

Despite his skill, Funakoshi was reluctant to accept challenges to fight. He believed karate was too dangerous to be used against another person, and thought the best way to learn was to practice the series of moves known as the *kata*. One of his proudest moments was the time his first two teachers – who had never praised him during training – congratulated him for avoiding a fight.

In time, word of karate spread to Japan, and in 1922 Funakoshi was invited to Tokyo to show his skills. So many people asked him for lessons that he decided to stay and teach there.

Funakoshi believed karate could get students ready for life, but he laughed at the silly claims of some so-called masters. He was skeptical of stories about smashing stones with bare hands, and stressed that this was not the point of karate anyway. "Those who take pride in breaking boards or smashing tiles," he said, "... really know nothing about karate. They are playing around in the leaves and branches of a great tree, without the slightest concept of the trunk."

The Birth of Judo

From combat to co-operation

Armed with his swords, the samurai was a fierce opponent. But what happened if an enemy managed to disarm him? Then he counted on his training in ju-jitsu (joo-jit-soo). This martial art helped the samurai defeat his attacker with as little force as possible, by using his opponent's own strength against him. From the 1000s to 1300s many schools of ju-jitsu were started, where samurai learned grappling moves and strikes to vital areas. Many samurai – especially masterless ronin – started their own schools in this style of self-defense.

But over time ju-jitsu got a bad reputation. It was used by gangs, bodyguards, or even bouncers in road-houses to control rowdy customers. In the late 1800s, Jigoro Kano tried to change this for the better.

Kano began learning ju-jitsu as a teenager, and it had improved his poor health. As he trained, he noticed that each master taught a bunch of techniques but that there was no single principle to connect them all in a way that made sense. Kano looked closely at the different schools of ju-jitsu to find the single most important idea behind all the moves. And at last he discovered it: to use your mind and body in the most efficient way you can. Kano's favorite saying was "minimum effort – maximum efficiency." In all things use the right amount of energy – no more and no less than you need – to accomplish a goal.

He kept ju-jitsu techniques that met this rule and threw out those that did not. His goal was to remake the great samurai art into something positive and non-violent. The result was judo, which means "gentle (or flexible) way." The idea behind judo is to give way to

Kano used the image of the willow tree to explain judo. The willow's branches are light and spring back when pushed. If they were heavy and stiff, snow and wind would break them. But because they bend along with these forces, the tree can survive greater storms than a sturdy oak.

Kano saw judo as Japan's gift to the world. Today it is practiced by millions of people. Only soccer has more countries in its international federation.

an attack while keeping your own balance. If a larger person pushes you and you push back, you will be knocked over. But if you yield just as much as she has pushed, and keep your balance, she will lose hers. Judo also makes use of leverage to even the odds between a small person and a large opponent.

Today, judo is pretty much the same wherever you go; it is not divided into many schools as with other martial arts. Students, called judoka, first learn how to fall safely. Next they learn how to grip their opponent's clothing for a throw, and they practice strong stances and footwork. Only then do they start to work on foot, leg, and hip throws, as well as locks and holds for grappling on the mat.

For Kano, judo was a way of life, and he believed its ideas could make you a better person. "Minimum effort – maximum efficiency" can be used outside the training hall, too. It might keep you from overreacting to a hot-headed person, or from losing your temper.

Kano also believed that co-operation was key to learning judo. Students should help each other to learn, not work against each other in a competitive way. He taught his students that a judoka trained half for herself and half for society.

Aikido

To injure an opponent is to injure yourself. To control aggression without inflicting injury is the Art of Peace.
– Morihei Ueshiba

In search of harmony

Sometimes a new martial art is born when a master combines old systems or looks at them in a new way. This is how the Japanese art of aikido (eye-kee-doh) came to be. Its name means "way of harmony with the ch'i," the special energy in all living things.

A young man named Morihei Ueshiba was such a keen martial arts student that he trained in many styles – including ju-jitsu, kenjitsu, and judo. He was a big admirer of Japan's traditional martial arts, but he wished there was a style based on harmony, not competition or violence. As he trained, his ideas about the martial arts became more and more spiritual. In time, Ueshiba became a martial arts teacher himself, and through the 1920s and 1930s his new ideas took shape as aikido.

Aikido has a lot in common with the soft, internal martial arts. An aikido expert defends himself with circular movements and avoids an attack by shifting his body. As in judo, he uses an attacker's own force against him. Ueshiba believed that harmony is always better than confrontation. When two opposite forces meet, they clash and create violence. But if you don't resist a force, you can direct its energy where you like. Today, police in many countries study aikido because they can use it to control a violent person during an arrest. Still, there is much more to aikido than self-defense. Ueshiba's life was a long search for truth and self-knowledge. For him, the "path" of aikido never ended.

Morihei Ueshiba used images and poetry to teach the ideas behind aikido. "Depending on the circumstance, you should be hard as a diamond, flexible as a willow, smooth-flowing like water, or as empty as a space."

From Monks to Movie Stars

The martial arts come to the West

For a long time the martial arts stayed a well-kept secret in Asia. It was rare for anyone from the West to know about them, never mind train in them. This all changed around the mid-1900s.

During the Second World War, soldiers from North America and Europe spent time in Japan and Okinawa, and saw first-hand the skills of martial artists. They were impressed! When the war ended, some of those soldiers invited martial arts teachers to return home with them, and so Japanese arts such as judo and karate spread to the West. In much the same way, soldiers from the West got to know Korea's martial arts during the Korean War of the 1950s.

Workers from China came to the United States as early as the mid-1800s to work in the mines during the gold rush. But those who were martial artists usually kept their talents a secret. Then, in the twentieth century, more and more people from China began to move to North America, and they brought along their skills in the many styles of wushu. At first the Chinese masters taught only Asian students, and they often continued old traditions of secrecy inside their community.

Most North Americans got their first look at the martial arts in movies from Hong Kong and Hollywood.

The connection between acting and the martial arts is older than you might think. The steps and arm movements of Chinese opera often remind people of martial arts – and this is no coincidence. When the Shaolin monks were hunted by China's rulers, some of them hid out in the Peking opera. Today some opera actors begin training in martial arts at the age of six, to get their bodies ready for the tough demands of Chinese opera. Martial artist and actor Jackie Chan started training in opera when he was seven, and Bruce Lee's father was also an opera actor.

Some of the martial artists in these films became stars. Probably the best known was Bruce Lee, whose films made "kung fu" popular in the late 1960s and early 1970s. A little later, David Carradine played a Shaolin monk wandering through the U.S. in the 1970s TV series *Kung Fu*. Once the kung fu craze ended, American Chuck Norris – who trained in Korean tang soo do – helped make karate one of the most popular martial arts in North America. In recent years, Chinese stars Jackie Chan and Jet Li have shown North Americans their wushu skills in action movies.

Movies have made the martial arts very popular, but what they show is not always realistic! Scenes are often full of showy moves, making the martial artist look like a talented fighter above all else. The long fights are carefully staged to look exciting, and they sometimes exaggerate what a martial artist can do – which seems almost magical if you forget all the training behind every move. Bruce Lee once pointed out that real contests are over quickly. In fact, he had to slow down his movements so the audience could see them! The philosophies behind the martial arts might be mentioned in a film, but often only to give an "Eastern" twist to a traditional Western story of good guys fighting bad guys.

The way of no way

Bruce Lee (1940–73) created his own style of martial arts: jeet kune do, "the way of the intercepting fist." He liked to call his system the way of no way, and had very untraditional advice for his students: Don't be afraid to "steal" good techniques from other styles. Throw out what doesn't work for you, and add your own touches.

Lee did not teach set forms or techniques, but encouraged students to discover their own unique style. To do this, it was important to spar with experts from other kinds of martial arts, not just wushu. Lee also rejected other traditional ideas about martial arts, such as teaching only Asians.

Hong Kong has produced countless martial arts movies since the 1950s. Today they are big business, both in China and in Hollywood.

The legend of wing chun

Most people would be surprised to hear that Bruce Lee's first martial art was invented by a nun!

When he was thirteen, Bruce Lee began training in the wushu style known as *wing chun*, which means "beautiful spring." This self-defense style is full of quick punches and low kicks.

According to legend, wing chun was created when China's rulers turned against the Shaolin monks. The head monks realized they needed a new fighting system – one the government soldiers didn't know and that they could teach quickly to the new people joining their cause. But before they could finish developing this secret style, the Shaolin Temple was burned by its enemies. A Buddhist nun named Ng Mu was one of the lucky few to escape, and while she hid out, she finished perfecting the new martial art. Her first disciple was a young girl she called Yim Wing Chun.

In another legend, Ng Mu taught Yim Wing Chun the new martial art to save her from being forced to marry a man she didn't love. Ng Mu asked the powerful suitor to wait a year before the marriage. She used this time to train the young girl in her secret martial art. When the year was up, Ng Mu told the man that Yim Wing Chun was a martial artist and could marry someone only if he could defeat her in a match. Seeing how small the girl was, the suitor smiled and agreed. But Yim Wing Chun defended herself with such speed and skill that he could find no way to defeat her, and had to accept that the marriage was off.

Martial Arts Enter the World of Sports

As the martial arts became more and more popular around the world, they headed in a new direction. Competitions – with rules and judges – sprang up everywhere, and some martial arts started to look more like modern sports. Students got a chance to test their skills, and spectators had exciting matches to watch. But the new focus on sport changed many martial arts in important ways.

Contests were not always a big part of the martial arts. Before 1940, sparring was not even allowed in Okinawan karate. Masters believed it was enough to train in the basics and then perfect your skills with form practice. No one thought of karate as a sport. But once karate spread through Japan, sparring became more common in training, and the "sport" of karate – an idea started by some of Funakoshi's students in the 1930s – became popular.

Today you'll find two kinds of martial arts: traditional ones that practice the old ways and competitive arts that have become sports. Judo became an Olympic sport in 1964, something its founder, Jigoro Kano, worked to make happen. But some say that Kano's ideals have been changed along the way. For Kano, judo was about co-operation, and he discouraged students from competing with one another. Yet in today's judo matches, points are awarded for being aggressive, even though this goes against Kano's teachings – not to mention the principles behind most martial arts.

So does competing make people lose sight of the real martial spirit? Some teachers suggest balance is the key. Competitors can keep co-operation a part of their martial "way" by taking time to help out junior students in their club, for instance.

Championships bring the martial arts to a wide audience and give young students heroes to look up to. But the glitter of medals can make it hard to remember the most important goals of the martial arts.

That Was Zen, This Is Now

How the West changed martial arts

Whenever the martial arts traveled somewhere new, they not only changed the people who learned them but were changed themselves. As they passed from Chinese monks to Okinawan fishermen to Korean nobles, each new home gave them a different shape. And this is also true of the martial arts since they have come to the West. Traditional Asian masters might not recognize some of today's classes!

Movies and the Olympics got lots of people interested in the martial arts. The fight scenes on the screen were so impressive that people wanted to learn the moves for themselves. Many signed up for classes – but they expected something very different from traditional martial arts training. They had seen what a trained body could do but didn't understand the total way of life that the martial arts were supposed to be. For most people in the West, the martial arts were one of two things: a way to defend yourself or a sport to compete in. Few people knew about the philosophies behind the martial arts; they saw only moves that could be useful. But the martial arts have always been more than this.

Many beginners wanted to learn

Movies can give people the wrong idea about martial arts. They're not about learning to fight on the street.

At class, martial arts students bow to show respect – to an opponent, an instructor, or a senior student.

self-defense and hoped to see fast results, so some teachers began to offer what students wanted. They advertised self-defense classes, and held contests to impress the public with displays of strength and speed. While this attracted new students, it did nothing to teach one of martial arts' basic lessons – to be modest and not brag about skills!

This new kind of school sold students things they could see: belts of different colors to show their rank, self-defense moves, medals from competitions. Less time was spent helping students work on their minds and characters. Meditation might be used in class, but often it was a tool to help students concentrate on the moves they were about to make or think about their performance.

Can East meet West?

Ways of teaching the martial arts also changed once they came to the West. For instance, a traditional Asian master might teach you a move by showing it to you instead of telling you what to do and placing you in the right position. This way, you would have to think to copy him, instead of just listening to instructions.

Traditional masters also expected a lot of discipline and patience from students. If a teacher in the West tried to do the same, he would probably see a lot of students drop out.

In fact, even if someone wanted to, it would be hard to teach in the traditional way in the West. People have different ideas about teachers and students – and different ways of thinking about themselves and the world. But some schools do find a balance in the way they teach. Studies have shown that when a school teaches something about a martial art's philosophy and history, students are less likely to fight or use their skills to hurt others.

Martial Arts Today

Today's martial arts schools – often called dojos – have their roots in very old traditions but have also changed with the times. You might find yourself kicking or grappling with a group of students in all sorts of places: a school gym, a community center, a commercial club, or even a park.

Kids in Martial Arts

Today people all over the world practice the martial arts – and many of them are kids. In China, kids often learn wushu as part of their physical education at school. Kendo and judo are popular choices with young people in Japan, and judo is also a big martial art in Europe. Kids in North America are taking up all sorts of martial arts styles, karate and tae kwon do being among the most popular.

Why do they study the martial arts? The benefits that Bodhidharma's monks got from training are still valuable today: a healthy body, a sharp mind, and the feeling that you are working toward your personal best. Now as then, training can help you learn about yourself and what you can do. It can also help you to think and react quickly in all sorts of situations.

While beginners might have unrealistic ideas about martial arts, training often sets them straight. Studies have shown that the longer kids train, the less aggressive they get, and the more self-control and discipline they have.

What's more, students in martial arts often find they get more confident and are less likely to let others make them feel mad or pushed around. Co-operation is important in many classes, since it takes two willing partners to learn a throw! Kids also get a chance to be leaders and teachers, especially as they advance through the ranks and start helping beginners in their club.

Many martial artists believe that what you learn in a dojo can come in handy in the rest of your life. Take reflexes, for example. Have you ever caught a falling glass before it hit the ground? Or, on the other hand, did you watch it fall and break before you could react? Quick reflexes take practice. The same is true of alertness. Martial training helps people become more aware of their surroundings – and of potential dangers. In some classes, students are asked to close their eyes and describe who is sitting next to or behind them, so they can sharpen these skills.

Think fast!

Gichin Funakoshi, the founder of modern karate, gave karate credit for his skills in other parts of life. He was good at stopping arguments and helping people come to an agreement. His quick reflexes even saved his life. While boarding a large ship from a small boat, he was caught with one leg on each when a big wave rocked both vessels. Funakoshi couldn't swim, but in a flash he shifted his briefcase from one hand to the other. The weight gave him the momentum he needed to carry him safely onto the ship.

Another useful skill is concentration. You need to focus to remember all the parts of a *kata* as you move through it – and being able to think about one thing until it's finished is a skill anyone can use outside the dojo.

Some martial arts teachers have noticed that their students reach a balance. Kids with quick tempers or pushy ways tend to become calmer and more easygoing, as training gives them a way to use their energy. And shy kids come out of their shells as they gain confidence in their skills.

While there are many good reasons for trying the martial arts, there are also some not so good ones. Anyone looking for fast results or a quick fix to a problem will soon realize that training in the martial arts takes patience and lots of practice. And those who want to learn to fight will quickly find that good schools teach non-violent ways of acting and of staying safe.

Today's Dojos

Kids of different sizes and ages line up across a mat, facing a wall of mirrors. Their white jackets are tied with belts ranging from white to yellow to orange. In front of them is a karate instructor – their "sensei" in Japanese – who will lead them through some brief meditation, followed by warm-ups and then *kata*. While their sensei leads the class, assistant instructors give one-on-one advice as they move through the students.

All the special clothes and bowing that are part of a dojo may seem mysterious at first, but everything has a reason, often based on tradition. The loose-fitting jackets and pants worn in karate, tae kwon do, and judo are like the clothes worn centuries ago in Asia. In the same way, the gear worn in kendo is based on samurai armor, but changed to be comfortable today. Bowing shows respect for the teacher, fellow students, and the school itself – demonstrating that it is more than just a gym to play around in. Students often bow as they arrive at or leave the practice area.

Form practice – *kata* in Japanese – is a basic part of classes for many martial arts, including karate, tae kwon do, and wushu styles. Practice with a partner is a big part of arts such as judo. There are classes for beginner, intermediate, and advanced levels, but some schools have mixed-level classes – where advanced students set an example for beginners. Sometimes adults and kids train together in family classes. And kids often move into adult classes once they reach their teens.

Some schools even arrange student trips to the birthplace of their martial art. Or they might have exchanges with teachers from Asia, inviting them to come teach a special class for the kids in the school.

Competitions are one way students can test their progress. Some martial artists feel that contests don't fit in with

> Today the black belt is worn by martial arts students who have reached a high level of skill. But the different-colored belts used to show rank are a fairly new idea. Long ago, all belts were white, but after much use they would get dirty and become darker. In time, a dark belt came to be a sign of an experienced martial artist.

the traditional goals of co-operation and avoiding fights. But other teachers encourage kids to at least try competitions to face whatever fears they might have about them. Competitions do have benefits: students get to meet new opponents they've never practiced with before, who have different ideas and training. This can help them improve and learn more about their own strengths and weaknesses.

This is one common sequence for karate belts, but other martial arts styles have their own colors and ranks.

Colored belts are often awarded as a symbol of how much a student has learned – and to give kids something to work for. Beginners start with a white belt and move up through different colors all the way to black. In karate, for example, you might learn a new *kata* and pass a test to get to the next belt. The number of belts and colors changes with different martial arts and sometimes with different schools, but ten belt levels up to black is pretty common. Not all martial arts use belts, though. Internal styles such as tai chi don't rank progress in any obvious way – it's something you and your teacher can see happening.

The time it takes to move from one belt to the next depends on the student, but it is usually at least a few months. In many karate schools, a beginner can expect to take four or five years to move up to a black belt. While some schools have a minimum age for the black belt – say, 16 – others feels this just discourages younger kids.

It might seem that once a student earns the black belt, she knows everything. But most black-belt students are quick to point out how much they have left to learn! For many, the black belt is a new beginning, and with it comes a duty to represent their martial art to the rest of the world.

Starting Out

What's the best age to start the martial arts? The youngest kids in a school are often five or six, but some kids begin as young as three! What's more important than age is being interested and finding a program that's right for your age group. You will find beginners of all ages – from kids to seniors – in martial arts schools.

Once you've decided to start, how do you choose from the many styles? Each one offers something different, so it helps to learn all you can about them. What appeals to you? The punches and shouts of a karate *kata*? Working with partners to perfect judo throws? The weapons and rituals of kendo? Or maybe the flowing movements of tai chi? Keep in mind that internal schools offer less obvious rewards and ranks than, say, karate or tae kwon do. They are about inner progress rather than belts.

Next, how do you go about finding a good school? A Chinese saying warns that it is better to spend three years looking for a good teacher than three years studying with a bad one!

For many martial arts there is no guaranteed "certificate" that instructors can show you to prove they are good teachers. Official organizations for each style may be able to recommend a school in your area, or friends might tell you about a class they liked.

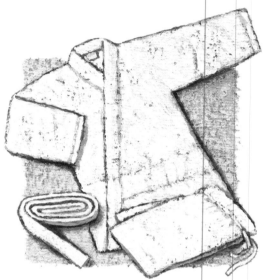

Martial arts students often wear special clothing in class. The most common uniform is the "gi," a white jacket and loose pants. Karate, judo, and tae kwon do each have their own version of the gi.

But the best way to judge is to see for yourself. Visit the school and watch a class, or take a trial class if you can. Are the kids enjoying themselves? And are their families watching in an area set aside for them? Look on the dojo wall for certificates showing the instructor's rank, title, and association (they're often at the front, or "shomen,"

Make the entire universe your dojo. This is the great meaning of the martial way.
– Morihei Ueshiba, founder of aikido

of the dojo). And talk to the instructor. If the martial art uses a ranking system, he or she should be a black belt – but there is more to know than this. How long did she study and how long has she been teaching?

Finally, what are the school's ideas about the martial arts? Do they promise only self-defense skills, ignoring the other parts of the martial arts way? The best schools try to strike the balance that is the key to following any "do" or "way" – giving their students the chance to grow in mind, body, and spirit.

Glossary

Aikido: The "way of harmony with the ch'i." A defensive Japanese martial art founded by Morihei Ueshiba in the 1930s. It uses quick movements to turn an attacker's force against him.

Black belt: A sign that a martial artist has reached an expert level. It is awarded in some martial arts, including karate, judo, and tae kwon do. The black belt itself is usually divided into ten ranks, known as "degrees" or "dan."

Bodhidharma: Buddhist monk from India who, according to legend, taught martial arts to the monks at China's Shaolin Temple in the AD 500s.

Buddha: A title that means "enlightened one," given to honor the founder of the religion Buddhism.

Bushido: "The way of the warrior." The samurai code of conduct and way of life.

Ch'i ("ki" in Japan and Korea): The vital energy in all living things. Many martial arts aim to increase the amount of ch'i in the body.

Confucius: Chinese philosopher who lived from 551 to 479 BC. His ideas about morals, politics, and society came to be known as Confucianism.

Do: Japanese word for *way*. It describes a martial art that is a path toward becoming a better and wiser person. For example, tae kwon do, judo, kendo.

Dojo: Training hall where martial arts are taught.

Enlightenment: The goal of Zen meditation, when a person briefly "sees" the basic truth of things. Known as "satori" in Japan.

Hard, external styles: Martial arts that use strikes and straight-line movements. Shaolin Temple boxing and karate are examples.

Jeet kune do: The "way of the intercepting fist." A martial art style created by wushu master and actor Bruce Lee in the 1960s. It has no set forms; each student develops her own style through experience.

Judo: The "gentle way." Japanese martial art based on ju-jitsu, developed by Jigoro Kano in the late 1800s. This defensive style aims to put an opponent off balance with throws and grappling moves.

Ju-jitsu: Japanese martial art that dates back to samurai schools of the 1100s to 1300s. It uses grappling and strikes to vital areas to stop an attacker.

Karate: "Empty hand." Martial art from the island of Okinawa that first developed sometime before AD 1400. It was later introduced to Japan by Gichin Funakoshi in 1922. In this hard style, strikes and blocks are made by the hands and feet.

Kata: Japanese word for the series of movements a martial artist practices during training.

Kendo: The "way of the sword." Japanese martial art that grew from samurai sword fighting (kenjutsu). Wooden or bamboo swords are used, and skill and technique are more important than strength.

Kung fu: "Learned skill." A Chinese term used in the West as a name for many different Chinese martial arts.

Lao-tzu: Founder of the philosophy of Taoism, who lived in the 500s BC. He is said to have written the *Tao-te Ching*, "The Way and Its Power."

Ninja: "One who steals in." Japanese martial artist who was hired to carry out missions of sabotage, spying, or tricking the enemy.

Ninjitsu: The art of the ninja. It included empty-hand martial arts, weapons training, disguises, and escape techniques.

Philosophy: A system of thought and action that offers a way of looking at the world and a person's place in it. Important philosophies for the martial arts are Zen Buddhism, Taoism, and Confucianism.

Samurai: "One who serves." Japanese warriors who formed the ruling class from the 1100s to mid-1800s.

Sensei: The Japanese word for "teacher." It is a term of respect for a martial arts instructor. Another title is *shihan*, which means "master instructor."

Shaolin Temple: A Buddhist monastery in China, the legendary birthplace of Asian martial arts.

Shaolin Temple boxing: Hard martial art that grew from the exercises Bodhidharma taught the monks.

Soft, internal styles: Martial arts that use circular, defensive movements to avoid an attack. Tai chi chuan is an example.

Sun Tzu: Chinese author of *The Art of War*, one of the first books on military strategy. He believed strategy was more important to victory than strength.

Tae kwon do: The "way of the foot and fist." Korean martial art that was created in 1955 but based on older Korean styles, in particular subak. Like karate, it uses strikes with the hands and feet. It is also famous for high, jumping kicks.

Tai chi chuan: "Grand ultimate fist." A soft, internal martial art that uses flowing, circular movements to control the flow of ch'i in the body.

Taoism: "Following the way." A philosophy based on the teachings of Lao-tzu.

Wing chun: "Beautiful spring." A defensive Chinese martial art created by Ng Mu, a Buddhist nun of the Shaolin Temple. It uses quick, straight punches and low kicks.

Wushu: "War arts." In China, a general term for all Chinese martial arts.

Yin-yang ("in-yo" in Japan): Chinese symbol of opposites in balance. *Yin* stands for ideas such as negative, soft, and dark; *yang* stands for positive, hard, and light. Taoism and many martial arts teach that it is important to balance these opposites.

Zen ("Chan" in China): A sect of Buddhism, brought to China from India by Bodhidharma. It teaches that meditation is the way to enlightenment, and has been an important part of many martial arts.

Index

We acknowledge the support of the Canada Council for the Arts, the Ontario Arts Council, and the Government of Canada through the Canada Book Fund (CBF) for our publishing activities.

ONTARIO ARTS COUNCIL
CONSEIL DES ARTS DE L'ONTARIO

Cataloging in Publication
Scandiffio, Laura
   The martial arts book / by Laura Scandiffio ; art by Nicolas Debon.

Includes index.
ISBN 978-1-55037-777-4 (bound).—ISBN 978-1-55037-776-7 (pbk.)

   1. Martial arts—Juvenile literature. I. Debon, Nicolas, 1968- II. Title.

GV1101.35.S23 2003 j796.8 C2002-904336-0

The art in this book was rendered in mixed media.
The text was typeset in Angryhog ITC, Charlotte, and Slimbach.

Distributed in Canada by Firefly Books Ltd.
66 Leek Crescent
Richmond Hill, ON L4B 1H1

Published in the U.S.A. by Annick Press (U.S.) Ltd.
Distributed in the U.S.A. by Firefly Books (U.S.) Inc.
P.O. Box 1338
Ellicott Station
Buffalo, NY 14205

Printed and bound in China.

Visit us at: www.annickpress.com

Acknowledgments

I wish first of all to thank Rick Wilks of Annick Press for giving me the opportunity to write this book, as well as Sheryl Shapiro for her thoughtful design and helpful suggestions. Many thanks to the martial arts instructors who took time to answer questions and invited me to watch classes, in particular David Miller of the Canadian Judo Academy, Michael Walsh of Northern Karate Schools, and Andy James and Colin Outram of the Tai Chi and Meditation Centres. I would also like to express my appreciation to Professor W. Dan Hausel, 9th Dan, of the University of Wyoming Shorin-Ryu Karate and Kobudo Club for reviewing the manuscript and providing helpful comments and answers to questions.

For Rob
—L.S.

To Sifu Ali Siadatan
—N.D.